INTAGLIO

WICK POETRY FIRST BOOK SERIES
Maggie Anderson, Editor

Already the World
Victoria Redel   Gerald Stern, Judge

Likely
Lisa Coffman   Alicia Suskin Ostriker, Judge

Intended Place
Rosemary Willey   Yusef Komunyakaa, Judge

The Apprentice of Fever
Richard Tayson   Marilyn Hacker, Judge

Beyond the Velvet Curtain
Karen Kovacik   Henry Taylor, Judge

The Gospel of Barbecue
Honorée Fanonne Jeffers   Lucille Clifton, Judge

Paper Cathedrals
Morri Creech   Li-Young Lee, Judge

Back Through Interruption
Kate Northrop   Lynn Emanuel, Judge

The Drowned Girl
Eve Alexandra   C. K. Williams, Judge

Rooms and Fields: Dramatic
Monologues from the War in Bosnia
Lee Peterson   Jean Valentine, Judge

Trying to Speak
Anele Rubin   Philip Levine, Judge

Intaglio
Ariana-Sophia M. Kartsonis   Eleanor Wilner, Judge

Intaglio

Poems by

Ariana-Sophia M. Kartsonis

The Kent State University Press

Kent, Ohio

© 2006 by Ariana-Sophia M. Kartsonis
Library of Congress Catalog Card Number 2006011516
ISBN-10: 0-87338-891-7
ISBN-13: 978-0-87338-891-7

Manufactured in the United States of America

10 09 08 07 06   5 4 3 2 1

The Wick Poetry Series is sponsored in part by the Stan and Tom Wick
Poetry Center at Kent State University.

LIBRARY OF CONGRESS CATALOGING-IN-PUBLICATION DATA
Kartsonis, Ariana-Sophia M., 1966–
    Intaglio : poems / by Ariana-Sophia M. Kartsonis.
        p.   cm. — (Wick poetry first book series)
    ISBN-13: 978-0-87338-891-7 (pbk. : alk. paper) ∞
    ISBN-10: 0-87338-891-7 (pbk. : alk. paper) ∞
    I. Title.   II. Series.
PS3611.A7848I67 2006
811'.6—dc22   2006011516

British Library Cataloging-in-Publication data are available.

For my parents: My father, George, for his constant love & faith.
My mother and best friend Kathryn.
And for their mothers, Asemoula and Olga.

CONTENTS

Acknowledgments   ix

Foreword by Eleanor Wilner   xi

I

Caravansary   3

Vanishing Armenia   4

Alluvial Liturgy in Crayon   8

Fernando Pessoa, I Salute You All!   10

Harem Girl   13

Cisterna   14

Epithalamium Fifty-five Years after the Fact of Your Saddest Day   16

Lunacy   18

Obligato   19

Shaping the Spoon   21

Flamenco   23

Limbo   25

1963 Photograph of My Mother, Ekaterena, at Nineteen, a Bride   27

Litote, Smoke Trees, Fireworks over Water   29

A Hummingbird Feeder Shaped Like a Strawberry   32

{   41

II

Lathe   45

When Playing by the Blues   47

Blues Turned to Bruise   48

Making Red   51

Caddis Flies in Two Lessons   52

What It Took to Look Away   54

Reconstructing a Bird   55

The Dead Magician's Things   57

Sigh   60

Contre-Coeur   61

Romance in Celadon   63

Any Old Miracle   65

Hot Lunch Poem   66

Intaglio   69

Bridge of Sighs   72

Black Powder   74

III

Marina Tsvetayeva Responds to a Present-day Paramour Writing
    from the French Quarter   77

Found Poem, Lost Girl, 1918   78

Ordinary Heartbreak   79

Dear Rainer Maria Rilke,   81

The Today Wounded One   82

Nearer Venus   83

Marina Responds to Her Eldest Daughter   85

I Absolve You, Marina Tsvetayeva   86

Reasons I Gave for Giving It Up   89

Castanet   90

Damasked   92

Eulogy for a Mourning Cloak Butterfly   93

Glean   94

Notes   96

ACKNOWLEDGMENTS

Special thanks, too:

My wonderful sisters: Antonia, good reader, bright, kind believer in all this pineapple calligraphy; Christina, my better echo, my Lightning Bug. My uncles, Johnny and Elias Pavlos.

Of course, to Eliot Wilson, *true* friend. To Prabhakar Kudva: Patron (saint) of the arts. And to Cynthia Saeli for her giant heart (plus, her N.Y. apartment that saved my sanity more than once). Kathrine Wright, Liz Besmehn—choice sisters, sister-scribes. Simone Muench. Maggie Hermes. Steph Rogers: a year of ashes and ballads. Lesley Jenike (& you too, Josh Butts, filo of mine), Cindy King, Nancy Bauman, Holly & Peter Karapetkova for that summer. Ander Monson, Alicia Holmes, Matt Guenette, Paul Guest, Abraham (deer boy) Smith, Bruce Spencer, Elizabeth Simpson (more than *semi*-precious), and to Alexander Sartwell for elegance, eloquence, friendship, beautiful meals, and the story for *Black Powder*. For her enthusiasm and her own fine poems, *Vanishing Armenia* goes out to Diana der Hovanessian. For laughter again, Caleb Adler.

To Jacqueline Osherow, for her poems and crucial friendship; also Magda, Dora, Mollie, and Saul for being my downtown family—*thank you*. François Camoin, Robin Behn, Michael Martone, Bruce Smith, Don Bogen, John Drury, Joanie Mackowski. Jim Cummins: teacher, friend, conspirator, maker of mixed tapes, thank you for all that plus wicked humor.

Because it's been a long ride, I owe many thanks—some of which I've likely left off. So here's a general sweep of thank yous to the countless good readers of my work in my workshops at universities of Utah, Alabama, and Cincinnati. A special shout-out to the members of Write Angles—scattered now but remembered. My thanks to the Buford Boone family for their great name and the support in the form of a fellowship they provided for me at the University of Alabama. Likewise, to the (George) Elliston family for their support at the University of Cincinnati. To my students: from Utah to Alabama to Cincinnati—you inspire me daily—thank you. To the Wick Poetry Center, wise Maggie Anderson, and to Eleanor Wilner (with haloes to spare) for choosing this book and taking such time and care with it.

Finally, for Josh Bell somehow throughout.

· · ·

Major thanks to the editors of the journals in which these poems appeared, sometimes in slightly different forms: *Another Chicago Magazine, Colorado Review, Denver Quarterly, www.thediagram.com, Fine Madness, Florida Review, Flyway, Green Hills Literary Lantern, Gulf Coast, Indiana Review, Nimrod, Other Voices, Slope, Third Coast, West Branch, www.glimmertrain.org,* the *YWCA of Southhampton,* and *RUNES, A Review of Poetry.*

The image evoked by *Intaglio,* title of this first collection by Ariana-Sophia M. Kartsonis, rests on a paradox, one perhaps central to the poetic impulse itself: that design can be shaped by what is cut away, by the loss that surrounds it, so that what is missing creates the negative space which raises the figure in relief, presents it to sight and touch. Relief: a word whose two meanings—one artistic and material, the other emotional and intangible—together suggest how art engraves meaning.

But let us take the figure only as far as its usefulness extends—for though intaglio is the art of image accretion by subtraction, it scarcely hints at the plenitude of that accretion in these poems: the baroque lushness and sheer momentum of the lines, the associative rush of language like water over a spillway, the allusive layers of reference, the delightful prodigality of it all. This bountiful excess may seem an unexpected companion to an art so en-graved by loss, but such contradictions are in the nature of experience. Kartsonis uncovers this truth even in the visual resemblance of words, where eros is seen as the beginning of erosion—the unstoppable energies of desire linked to loss and attrition, even as these poems dispel gloom by the dazzle of language, its daring and vitality.

The epigraph for the collection places loss in a long context; the quotation is anonymous, its source the ancestral mothers who had neither public name nor voice: *At this time let me somehow bequeath all the leftovers to my daughters and their daughters.* This will be, then, a collection whose marrow is the mother-daughter bond under straitened circumstances, a legacy of making do with "leftovers," seen not in some narrowly personal way, but against a larger history—in this case, that of Greek-Americans, and from the vantage of an awakened, troubled daughter.

The mother/daughter nexus opens in a vastly different configuration later in the book, as Kartsonis considers a nontraditional pair: the vexed connection between the unmotherly, mercurial Russian poet Marina Tsveteyeva and her daughter Ariadna, written with a detailed knowledge of their lives that gives authority and richness to the posthumous voices of both women.

Marina/Ariadna usefully complicate the subject of how a mother's choices and condition impinge on the daughter whose identity depends on how consciously and creatively she understands and struggles both for and against her progenitor. Ariadna's ultimate forgiving of Marina ("I Absolve You, Marina Tsveteyeva"), that fury of creative energy, missing in the "mineral mother . . . granite woman" of tradition ("Glean"), becomes a liberating action for Kartsonis herself.

For she is, of course, also a poet, and one of the primary signs of the energy and autonomy of the daughter is the imaginative venture of her language, its freedom to play for whatever stakes its truths demand. Radically different stylistic approaches serve separate necessities, ranging from a wildly expressive and associative style of exfoliation to a more traditional construction—coherent progression, sequential syntax, a clear and trackable narrative—employed when the daughter interpretively recovers the past of the mother and grandmother, a style that recurs in some of the historical Marina/Ariadna persona poems.

A very different language emerges in the poems of her own present—driven by the internal pressures within, genii who are both in and out of the bottle: "With every bluejay feather he'll say: / *Soon we'll reconstruct a whole bird* / and I see it, bedraggled yet soaring / in a hush of glass-bottle blue." Here is an emblem of her intention, a kind of ars poetica: soaring within constraint, kaleidoscopic shifts of bright fragments, saturated dyes, blue feathers, bloody apricots, high energy, mixed dictions, sheer nerve, disturbed syntax, unlikely conjunctions; an equivocal project of reconstruction supercharges the language of loss, giving it generative force. With a metaphoric magician's sleight-of-hand, one thing becomes another: " . . . it's not the fireworks that move me / but the smoke after, when the night becomes / a kimono stitched in vines of used light," " . . . your mind a corset, my grandfather's fingers / too eager at the eyelet and hooks, entangling in the ribbon, / tearing at the netted lace"; abstractions take on weight and personality: "Joy, the last soul on board, misses her stop. / The past hunkers down for a smoke."

I want to end this introductory note by citing a poem, one of those that I find most moving and memorable in the collection, and one which seems appropriate to mention in relation to the grieving circumstances that brought the Wick Poetry Center and this, the Stan and Tom Wick Poetry Prize, into being—commemorating, as it does, the untimely deaths of two young cousins killed in separate automobile accidents. Kartsonis's poem, "The Dead Magician's Things," is for a student killed in his 19th year: "*Memorable*—his mother asked what I might recall / if I had any old papers of his and I could only retrieve / a roll sheet with his signature, something / magical to it now. Any ink in his living hand / a magic marker." Echoing Roethke's great sorrowing poem for his student Jane, she says: "I with no rights in this matter either . . . no more eloquence can reach / what I meant, or match her son."

But language is sometimes all we have left, and it is to its final inadequacy and its absolute necessity that these fine poems dedicate themselves. And in the spirit of that paradox, I recommend them to you.

INTAGLIO

I

At this time let me somehow bequeath
all the leftovers to my daughters and their daughters.
ANONYMOUS

CARAVANSARY

We were victims of the circus dance.
Painted and perfumed, trounced out and about,

we figure-skated on thin niceties
served up on water crackers with a side of brie.

We were hoteled like complimentary shoeshine mitts
polishing off the evening

from a bottle with a tiny ship inside.
We grieved the trapezists. They grieved

the possible sky. Ambassadors of altitude,
we cried, there are things realer than this

bellydance with gravity. The sign propped
in a plate glass storefront read: WE MAKE SKIMPY BRIDES.

If the issue at hand is love
then batter my heart you three-faced dog.

Batter my heart, deep-fry it,
serve it to the fire-eating lizard girl.

Tell your circusy self a word in the hand
is worth two if by the see-if-I-care.

No one gyrates anymore.
The globe spins stupidly alone.

So we circle in for the thrill.
Step right up, step right up, Madame Tsigana said.

*Pull from sundown every bloody apricot,
there's more everything ahead.*

VANISHING ARMENIA

All spring swallows enter your father's home,
through its crushed windows.
DANIEL VAROUJAN

I. If we met on the street
in a foreign language,
who would it belong to?

I've never tasted your language
except on the tongue
of one sweet Armenian boy
who told me, *Greek,*
Armenian, same thing.
I know he lied; we are both
a proud, proud people.
I know he meant the kiss to seal
the space and I let it.
And I know he told the truth too:
he meant the suffering
that sends us half into a grave
when someone dies.
We don't believe in quiet passage;
scream back, kick, claw,
Take this, we say, *Take that,*
and death obliges, takes everything,
comes back for more.
We hide where we can:

between the pine-scented sheets
of the book one man gave me as a gift,
the imaginary travel guide book I gave him.
Peering through trellised fingers,
we say we can't see each other.
We know better and still we love.

II. Summer, 1993, Kusadasi, Turkey
My little sister and I in Ephesus
on tour with old men, their anger
still smoking: *These are Greek ruins,*
now they charge us to look at them. Those Turks.

Five hours we wandered,
through shops and ruins,
ogled young Turkish vendors,
suede-bodied men.
No women anywhere.
Christina recalls the flinty look
in our father's eyes when she came home
and spoke of their beauty
(and they were dark fires
—in their eyes, dusty dark hair,
eyes like gold-lit-afternoon-lichen-mossy-forests).
They marched through our villages,
our father said.
Stone-eyed, amber and olivine,
(they are a half honey-colored people).
You dropped my heart,
they said to the tourist women
and we heard wrong, started looking
on the ground for a fallen hat.

His beauty felt like something alive,
my sister said on the bus back
to the ship we'd reboard to our father's country.
(She meant the doll seller, a young boy
holding a doll to the bus window
and calling out, *I give you*
beautiful girl, I give you.)

Understand this, our father said, *we don't forget.*
We slept heavily that evening,
woke sweat-drenched and thirsty,
woke dreamy-eyed with impossible cravings:
chocolate glass, breadfruit,
the so-slow sweetness of honey
against dusken shoulders.
We swallow hard and the taste stays.
I mean they were *lovely* men.

They cut our country like a big cake
a slice here, there, they devour us, our father said.

It was summer and we wore sheerness,
filmy skirts, floated down Turkish streets,
imagined invisible women
in the windows watching.
We wore a veil of that fine Ephesian dust home
as a second skin and we shimmied sticky-skinned,
our hands, our mouths full of honey.

Dreamed our father there, gentle,
gone suddenly fierce:

They will never be our people.
Anything but a Turk.
Bring me home anything. . . .

III. February 14, 1997
I was three years outside of this life,
moving from my hometown, my sisters,
one boy born on Valentine's Day,
all left behind.

I was three years outside of today,
a warm day for winter,
but *this* is the Valentine I dreamed:

a book of poems
by an Armenian woman
who wrote of your words
under a foreign moon,
a wild, foreign moon.

In this lighting, everything's foreign,
our words, this town,
the body of a lover returns
as the body of a poet
killed in a square
nearly a century ago.

It's like nostalgia before the fact,
before there's anything to long for.
Like using past tense for a thing
you'd only wished for.
I never knew, I never knew

I only know it's Friday, Daniel,
I want what I want: a heart

embroidered with *your* words,
a book that smells of his house,
just one of the stones
they used to bring you down.

ALLUVIAL LITURGY IN CRAYON

The house opens like a blouse.
This way the windows are jagged stars,
an inward drawn breath.

Draw the house correctly
so that even without them:
   the little mother in her triangle skirt,
   silly sad father in his hat, his mustache,
   the child, the child who holds
   a balloon holds its place
   in the air, a sky punched out
   donut-holed where string binds
   a small stick finger,
we know where they go,
the pathway leading there;
the flowers on their stupid stems,
two leaves will do, five petals
or the serrated teeth of tulips,
three in row, different colors
(make it cheery) wellness is measured
by these things: a doorknob, a chimney
sending smoke signals
to the neighbors about the hearth,
the controlled fire.

Daylight's ended, father's car is drawn
back to the driveway, the mommy draws a sigh,
the child, the child's drawn back indoors.

Black crayon blacks
out the clattering day,
fills the neighborhood
with rest. The riverine
sleepers Z-ing on rectangle
pillows with circle heads.

The moon you must draw
with a benevolent face.
No light must rive the night,
the nightful in their crooked beds.
Draw the covers back and there:

The house opens like a blouse.
The windows are jagged scars.

FERNANDO PESSOA, I SALUTE YOU ALL!

I want to take off with you, I want to go away with you,
with all of you at once.

ALVARO CAMPOS

Let's pinkie promise never to part
ourselves out just because we know what it means
to be many-ed as a hotel corridor.
Each chamber of our hearts
contains a different guest,
and as the case may be, Fernando, Fernando,
it's hard to say who you are
when everywhere there's evidence of someone else's
aftershave, someone's cigarette left burning
in the ashtray in another wing of you.
Nonetheless, you're my favorite octopod
and I'd run away with you, Baby.
We could be in Sicily by Sunday
some of ourselves wandering the city
before that early light gets all used up.
Others of us sleeping in or fingerprinting
the crowd which is just you and me, which is
just fine, since I'm aware that you're aware
that mankind's just another way of saying, *There's nobody home.*

You'll know what I mean when I tell you that I've been known
to find myself on a metro train inside myself where one
or the other of me has already taken the last seat
and this ride, yet again, I stand, holding the strappy
thing that makes me feel like a side of beef hanging heavy
and jostled from the walls while my city, my city, smears
the side windows and I'm just trying to stay upright.
The train is preferable to a crowd
of us packed into my little vehicle of catastrophe.
    If one of us drives too fast in the rain
how many of us slide into oblivion?

You're all about the static, the stations between stations. You,
you are every radio in every hotel
in all the cities that are you and you again.

I'll give myself a heteronym
the same as my beloved's favorite poet.
Every final couplet will read the same:
How do you like me now, Love?
How do you like me now?

I've had some time to think it over and
I'd like to wash your back in Portuguese,
comb your hair in Spanish, address
your every eyelash by a petname.

The sky is made of cardboard.
I adore corrugation, the ups and downs,
a sheet of cardboard's inner life:
zig-zag and heart monitor and some dark honey
eyes, you've got there, Fern (may I call you
Fern?) casting your vertebraed shadow everywhere.
I'd follow those tracks, I'd take
that train across the country and write every day
to the man who first checked your book out of the library
for me, and who loved me, like God's greatest maniac,
until I kissed the magic from his top hat
and now, there's nothing I can do but wait
for the previews to end and hope, hope
the feature film will begin and at least one of me
will have even a bit part. Therein lies the problem
with leading men, Fernando, the screen darkens
and attitude gets thrown. Let's take a bus of us
to the drive-in movie starring *you,*
co-starring *you,* written, produced, edited
by *you:* my gaffer, my key grip, my best boy
electric, my soundtrack, *my all.*

You, me, and Jesus, Baby, we're lousy with disciples.
Mine drag me around by the scruff of the neck
and when I ask whether it's bitch-love or cruelty
that motivates this mode of travel, they don't say a word.

Here, there, everywhere you. And isn't that my hoop skirt?
Your mouth makes moths cry. Little life, won't you wear
me again like you did last fall? We held ourselves up to each other
like lighters at a rock concert and then the swaying started
and all the little people in my head stood up and did the wave.
If you take the stage, I might just shatter.

Some nights some trees become candelabras and I can almost
see your brilliance thrumming an octopus of torchlight:
each star toasting the others, each other toasting the stars.

HAREM GIRL

Third wife he made me. Strung me in stone.
Citrine. Amethyst. Smokey Topaz. Garnet.
Third wife. Unheard wife. Hung from a half-gone throat.
Dark and murky one. The semiprecious one.
Unfirst. I am not the one to feel
a phantom limb's pain. The vaporous nothing
of fleshlessness that dreamt of bodying
the bones, that dreamt of most loved and real.
Sister to thin air. I am not a woman
with a lost leg or an amputated
arm that recalls holding him, holding jasmine
oil nights as sole wife, voidless and whole. Removed,
I am the ghost limb that dreamed there
a severed girl and ached for her.

CISTERNA

Well
Sister
there
will
be
water.

What are
those well-
wishers waiting to be?
Tell them you are already sister
to the meadow's meadowness, the song's songing. Will
you ask them where they're headed, then tell them *you're already there.*

There will be water there.
There will be water.
There will
be well
enough alone enough for all and thirsters
everywhere will drink and drink and be

well. Believe
me when I tell you there
are miracles and there are miracles. We saw you, Sister
Extravagance, walk on water. Whatever
weighed heavy only buoyed you then. You knew about well-
being when you hardly felt the will

to be. You are the living will
of every dragonfly, you worship the bee
and his honey-ache. You've known it well.
The honeysuckle that drew him there
is called Kissing-by-the-Gate. This body of yours is mostly water.
This body, Sister,

is called a field. This field, Sister,
has known floods and fires and maintains will
over the succulents and drinks up on holy water
every drop. Who blesses the kneeling bee,
his church of being? Our offering of pennies rolled down a hill.
    The wishing well,
the tithing, the copper cargo that paves the cellar of throat where there

gleams this knowing: We will be sisters and resisters.
    There are transistor
radios singing from the well, all this is radiating. The flower is a given.
The water is given. We are given. We are given over.

EPITHALAMIUM FIFTY-FIVE YEARS AFTER THE FACT OF YOUR SADDEST DAY

Widow to so much,
what you want
is your Greek village
where Gypsies washed in the sea,
bodies and clothes.

What you want is to wear one young boy's
crescent-muscled arms like a sweater
to ward off cold weather, the cold
man about to take you
to a snow-smothered
forever foreignness.

Your first name means something like silverness,
your maiden name a built-in tarnish deepening.
He with the cobbler's name will have you
metal-shod and heavy-gaited
down an aisle leading straight to wilderness
stripped of its silvery light and so mute
from this day forward.

Widow, too, to touch.
I mean silence on the inside.

You will not hold yourself steady
at the sight of him.
You do not feel drunk with the sly secret
that awaits you in the wedding bed.
Nothing in you will sway
in the sway of his sway.

Yiayia, wish it so that I could take you back
to the dressing room where they pinched your cheeks,
varnished you like kindling, wrapped you

in a satin gown so white it shadowed blue
and misted you with a gossamer shroud,
made it hard to know your own face
in the thick glass mirror.

You were more a spider's intended
than a bride, your back
a dumb length of chain
sewn in just under the skin,
              each link painfully plain.

LUNACY

You made me imagine a color
to miasma, to duskfire. I was just five,
your country foreign to me as your paper
pastries and their clove navels.
Your too-intricate language.
Your husband's phlegm-stained newspapers.
The bittersweet smoke of his cigars
and carbon and a smell of felt hats,
newsprint, and unwashed hair.
The weary shrug of your dresses,
noisy organdy and damask. The tang of sweat
embroidered in your body heat.

You created rivers and named them as you went:
Silver-haired River, Wise River, Lip River, the River of Ache
until I felt queasy and silken and beyond all that
water I could never learn to claim or churn.

You placed us on the map and then
spun the globe and paper snowflakes rained down.

We climbed from aftermath into the arms of fall.
You fed me dried leaves and the day began to turn somersaults,
the cartwheel of sun rolled back the stone of another day.

Even between monsoons you always slipped
away into sanity's satin pocket, lined with lucidity
to your next unlacing.

Once, I imagined your mind a corset, my grandfather's fingers
too eager at the eyelet and hooks, entangling in the ribbon,
tearing at the netted lace.

OBLIGATO
Telling Her to Die

Do that body throw
and rose apron chiffonade
with the wrong sky above.

You, a mite in the curdled clot
of cloudbroth, that sour soup
you spooned up until every drop

was in you and you were gone-away
in a brain meant for surfing
hellfire in bare feet. Head over heels

and none of it love. You got nothing
you ever wanted and so much otherwise.
So go now while the light's still waiting to turn

you back into that girl longdead who loved a place,
a boy, melon roses, the way her fingers chopsticked
against crochet and needlepoint. Her father's hopeless

eyes, even the hump in her mother's back.
Go now, down
the tunnel of your dream

about cloudsmoke
where you tell the long gone
    Beloved,

    I want a butter dress
    and you, a red
    cat, someplace to go

    and watch bell peppers grow
    hearty rooms where we might live,
    where summer doesn't give

us up for dead then keep us going
for nearly a century of zero-joy
where we marry misery buttoned-up

in the mean shirt of the wrong boy
who asked my father for our life
and that father with the helpless eyes
could only shrug a reply.

SHAPING THE SPOON

This is what she felt: buckle-end of her father's belt,
the dry-smacked kiss of a wooden spoon
against her back, her brother's hands touching her
wrong. In a basement, my mother—a splintered girl—would wait
thinking of their cold metal bodies in the silverware drawer all night.
She'd gather them, knives, forks, spoons, bring them to bed,
    tell them a story,

sleep with them, clattering at the foot of the bed when she'd stir.
Tucking the teaspoons in like babies, the up-tilt
of their oval faces, their slender-handled bodies warm. Then she slept
    through the night;
something in her craving a way to save something, even one spoon
from all she couldn't save herself: the terrible weight
        of night, the cold hardness pressing her.

Even spoon-faced babies, even cavemen begin here:
with a stone-carved ladle or so the anthropologist's story
goes. You, Spoon, most complete, nothing like the spaced-out
fork, all that light between its tines, what can it cradle? Here's the way
it went down: early man moved from you to fork, then knife, span-
        ned a great distance of appetite.

You hovered by the coffee at the reading that night:
the poet began by saying each of her love poems once held a knife,
    each story
        a blade. In the steel clink of flatware I hear
the armor of body against body. Armed, I too began with knives, Spoon,
        worked my way backwards, left
always with a bad taste in my mouth, dry, metallic, a bit like blood.
    The wait

for love was endless and whether the straight
    edge of emptiness, the serrated saw blade of night
that caught me or the sharp prongs of need, who can tell?

I hoped for you: round curves and holding, wished for you, waited to hear
what kept you; all the while her story, my story, history
    weighed me down. I held onto a pronounced hunger to spoon

out the past, dilute and distribute it, and that sustained me.
    My baby spoon
was engraved with the wrong time of birth on the handle.
    Doomed, I'm still late,
            all tardiness, missed appointments. Sometimes I want to start
over, in reverse, give you that foreshadowing baby spoon,
    Spoon of spoons, but what might
                            you want with it? Surely you'd prefer her
                    story instead: a child called Mourning who kept

utensils warm at her feet all through the night. Those stories
only circle back, create their own orbit, spin their own tales. Want
slips into catwalk pumps, flashy as a spoon dug hilt-deep into a tired heart.

FLAMENCO

Consider my mother's brave January.
And that it seems to come for the daughters earlier
as if waiting in her body
for the words meant for the mother:
A touch on the shoulder
A creepy man at a dance
May I cut in?

The Spanish parade
for the Virgin of the Macarena.
A diamond tear on her cheek.
The risqué dance—a lushness of breast
and hip. This is the brand of God
to be drinking.

Guapa! Guapa!
The people shout   *Beauty Beauty*

Making love, I find a lump beneath my arm
and for one week I'm flirting
with the perilous—the irony at handing myself over
to eros and thanatos in the same shaky breath.

What if this were it?
The unwanted paramour, his undesired shoulder tap
May I cut in?
His fingers spidering down my spine.
That game of tag   until finally this, You're it

I meant to learn to silversmith   to kiss a woman full on the mouth
     full of intent to sing something (even badly) in the presence of
     strangers   to tell you something you
don't even want to hear   To go   nowhere
whose name isn't oil in the mouth   *unguent*
Amphora: a vessel for the thirsty

a vase shaped something like a woman
    with her hands at her hips   *Cistierna*
Words silkily quenching a thirst
just over a lifetime long

LIMBO

1. I'm here to say it can be a holding place for years.

A halfway house for love worn-out.
A microscopic erosion   eros broken down
to its elemental grind
                        and grinding down.
Root word for desire and distribute.
God of love, a cupid strike which starts that erogation,
one arrow-tip bit of flesh at a time.
Arouse   to stir.
Erose   one bite mark
shaped like a bitter moon.

2. Be it Catholic waiting room
or back bend under bamboo pole
held waist-high like a jumprope between two people
        then lower
                        and lower
and lower.

3. Someone will say *love* and then hold you under pressure
underwater for years and years,
saying he wants to make sure you have a drink.
Saying she wants to see you swim.

4. I mean the body is a gothic arch, a wishbone held at that angle
so sharp it has to snap.

5. The broken beak of a living bird
more painful than quick-bitten nails
their raw luna-beds.

6. A ghost rises on the stairs like
    a bathtowel moon, apparition of cheap light
    and terrycloth

hovers there a shiver
and then falls to the unswept floor.

7. I mean, the broken beak of a bird that has to go on.
The snag and the ache and hurts to take in
what you need just to fill you.

1963 PHOTOGRAPH OF MY MOTHER, EKATERENA, AT NINETEEN, A BRIDE

1. Gospel Truths

She hasn't even begun to grieve
yet she believes these things:
    If a woman brushes by the altar,
    as she approaches the priest for Holy
    Communion, it is desecrated.
Never leave a cat in the room with a baby,
as the animal will jump on the infant's chest
and steal its last breath.
    No menstruating woman should enter
    the church: a bleeding woman is a dirty thing.
Nor should she immerse herself in water,
her body open as a yawn.
The sea will swallow her organs
in a single gulp.
    Spit in the palm of your hand
    after giving praise to discourage the casting
    of the evil eye.
Never let a woman stomp your grapes:
the wine will turn to vinegar.

She only half-listened, her heart running ahead
to a dark-haired bad boy named Raphael,
a rogue no doubt, but reparable
with the love of a good woman.

Meanwhile her father arranged her wedding
to the youngest son of a copper miner.

2. Kitchen Island

    My father, baby-faced, just twenty-one,
took one look at the copper mine on the hill
where he was to work at his father's side

in powdery Utah snow—cold and indifferent
as a sneeze of talcum—and shuddered. He worked one week,
cursing every freezing minute and looking
over the white expanse for the rhythm of waves
scrolled back and reoffered.
In the evenings, he asked the landlord to circle numbers
in the want ads where a man without fluency
might work indoors.
He opted then for the hot hours spent over the grease-
clotted grill of a trainside diner.
I came from an island, he told my mother.
I wanted to be warm again.

3. Something Borrowed, Something Blue

For now, the wedding photo—my mother
in a lacy white gown, my father waiting
for later, which will look nothing like the later
he's imagining now, but more like lust
standing bedside, knock-kneed in sad galoshes.
Nothing like the slow unlacing of expectation,
falling glitter or celestial music. Just some weary
bodies, one reluctant, the other
over-eager, the rhythm
too-new and off.

And anyway, there is no man named Raphael
coming to save my mother from quiet love.
There is a boy-faced man named George
    who doesn't look like *ironic* innocence
    or like he's affecting a nonchalant dark side,
    or Raphael with hellmaker hair, a shrug
    of leather on his back.

Just George, the cook turned ordinary prince
of her story.
But she won't know that yet.

LITOTE, SMOKE TREES, FIREWORKS OVER WATER

Gorgeous emptiness you've been here all along,
splintering off a flame-thrown night somewhere.

A red one first: a tasseled crimson pom-pom.
A green chrysanthemum spirits out then

sputters down. Then light rain strings lake to sky.
After, the kind that open like a hand,

sprinkle a slow handful of foil confetti.
Next, a gaslight crown spurts blue: volcanic

bloom, a gush of blood from a well-deep wound.
But, like the right dress, isn't it *so me*

that it's not the fireworks that move me
but the smoke after, when the night becomes

a kimono stitched in vines of used light.
I mean, a garden of them grew from nothing.

First, flowers made of fire. Afterwards, smoke.
The sky up there, the lake's other sky. Both

make the city brocade, then brocade in-
to a world reflected so there are two,

and not one of them habitable. This past
year's written out in the longhand up there.

What flowers now flowers in burnt air
punctuated with spent light, ash, cinder.

For emphasis, note: an orchid of smoke.
Exegesis: see us here below: footnotes

to the dandelion asterisks blown
just a moment ago. Just yesterday

wasn't it high noon? Wasn't vacancy
a motel's *yes?* The bedspread, the same blue

as our blue-faced sky freckled with starlings?
One face holds a skyful of lost balloons.

One night's a kimono with worlds repeated
in its pattern. I envy them: vanished

rings, pistils, roundels, palms, like I envy
geese for belonging to nothing but sky

and water. And now, white poppies burn off
the gunpowder sky. I wanted to wear it,

wrap the whole clothy mess around me, and walk
across the bridge, wearing ashes of roses,

smoke lilies, asters, the little village,
and the people dragging like a bridal train.

I am thinking of your mother dying
in that dark kimono robe that held slim

ornaments of history, odd villages,
embroidered cherry blossoms, peonies,

bamboo, and another plant that reminds me
of a smoke tree—those desert shrubs that slouch

in their aridity. That sky in the lake
must know the other sky this way. Inside

me is the pocket mirror of how you felt.
Her dying every day in a robe that held an Orient

of loss. I am the lake face spitting back
the smoke vineyard, the flashpowder moon,

the spangled, ghostly space we leave behind
threaded in smoke-white through the satin lake.

She pulled a used and tired sky around her
body and took worlds away with her.

A HUMMINGBIRD FEEDER SHAPED LIKE A STRAWBERRY

Why not this year, this grand piano of loss
and August: month I've begun to distrust
for what it plays badly, what it pockets, what it keeps.

I don't really want to talk about her death.
when all I ever wanted for her was this quiet.
I want to tell you about the hummingbird,

who took the greater part of summer to find me.
I watched the feeder for weeks, until that day:
the beating of wings so fast they seemed to disappear.

All that effort just to stay in place.
The easy metaphor of them, like her
they live for sugar and flowers and like that,

I'd been waiting too (any sweetness)
by the window, watching the feeder for a first glimpse for so long.
So that the first sighting startled me, the reverse reaction

of those who take sphinx moths for hummingbirds,
I think *insect* first: the body fragile and fine: a velvet bullet
between propeller wings—a frenetic stillness.

***

1926: Boris Pasternak writes to Marina Tsvetayeva: *I wished to go out-
side and see what one poet's thinking of another poet had done to the air
and sky.* You, Yiayia, were just fifteen, but your brothers heard the gos-
sip: *Odd girl, that one, the dowry must be astronomical, and her father,
a poor man, her mother, the hunchback. Her face is fair though, and she
has something of a figure. An old man might find some use for her.
The kitchen. The bed.*

***

She was my storm-dweller, my brave weather-girl
who lived past every forecast so
I could almost believe she wouldn't ever really go.

    Fifty pounds she was then
    and wearing a child's sleeper into
    her two-minute death. Her stopped heart

        sighing back—but she must have
        seen him there—the man she so clearly despised
        as he reached out from the hallway between

worlds—phantomed, beckoning
from the foot of the hospital bed,
where she stared with a rigid focus

    and spit his name *Yiorgio:*
    the husband given to her like a virus.
    Then she shook her head adamantly *NO!*

        and turned back, stayed another week.
        She'd returned, determined to keep
        at least one world between them.

***

Eight visits this hour. Dust with wings. I had been watching for
the fancy feathers of Anna's, the vermillion décolletage of a Ruby-
Throated, a Black-Chinned, a Cinnamon, or the rare, iridescent
Berylline but not my bird, my bird is the same color as the body of a
daddy long legs, like gathered dust. Just then, I'd never seen anything
lovelier.

***

Yiayia, it's been nearly four decades since your time in the mental hos-
pital and your days spent watching me and somehow I think I'm living
the other life for you, that the boy I met three Augusts ago was your

village boy regifted, two lifetimes later. He and I were children together in some memory that we as such, couldn't have actually made. Our respective childhood homes six states apart. So this must be the life you meant. Words to save you and love ridiculous, astonishing, *unprecedented,* a reconfiguration of all time before it. Even yours.

***

Forgive me if I had almost stopped believing
he would really leave. That I half-expected he'd stay,
his little body surely doomed to freeze.
Forgive me, if somewhere I hoped for him to stay
against his own survival.

***

We are each   in our own way
bad   for someone.
We are each   in a bad way
for someone   we each want

to know what Anne Bancroft meant
when she said the secret to her long marriage
was that each day when she heard the key in the door
she knew the party was about to begin.

I have known   days and doors   like that.
To see a festival   in someone. To be a festival   for someone.
To know   not one day tumbled   into place like that for her   feels

like the key in the music box turned and turned and the little tin barrel chiming out *Paris in the Spring.* A small pig holds a concertina and there's a lost childhood in the rosy cheeks, the porcelain eyes. To feel someone before we see him. To cross under a tree and know he passed beneath it moments ago. To be granddaughter to a woman who turned

her own death away to avoid the husband calling out to her from the
other side.

Do you love Papou? I'd asked nearly daily. She laughed a dark parody
of laughter.

Veh-vee, she'd say, *sure, I do.* I was only five but I understood sarcasm
this way first.

Felt the bone-china nights waiting between the twin beds of their
dismal bedroom

and the echo of the cries my mother heard through her childhood
walls when her father

reached through that corridor between beds to a wife who detested
his touch.

When I grew older I promised myself a double bed, a husband I
would want to keep inside, and the sweetest million mornings of
waking beside him.

***

Nearly eighty years later, your granddaughter would read the letter
from Boris to Marina and know precisely what he must have felt.
She would be in love with a boy who was a man-sized snow globe of
weathers, carnivals with your granddaughter pressed to the glass of
him—believing she never had to die. You would have lost the initial
euphoria at your husband's death, would have already taken the gi-
ant trunk filled with your stored youth back to the village so changed
you would ask to return to the States in only three months. Your
brothers having stolen the land your father left for you. That longed-
for-long-ago village boy—so gone, and you, an old woman now.

***

I should have watched for him, devoted all of Saturday to a last
look, instead I shopped for a gift for him—a feeder. I considered the
simple glass test tube variety, an extravagant pine gazebo, the stained
glass villa hung from a beaded cord, the apple red, strawberry one
like a green-wigged heart. I returned, poured the colored sugar water

into the second feeder at a time when he'd normally hover and dart
to and from the porch a dozen times in an hour and I waited until
night with my chair by the window.

***

    How many last things slide by me that way?
    Watching for the last of them and then undramatically
    when I look away they slip out of my life.

***

The heavens we invent for you begin on a flight from Salt Lake to
Cincinnati, and at thirty thousand feet my mother sees a soap-carved
scene in a meadow of clouds, over here a stand of white pines, dainty,
articulate even a rosebush of white and there, a bit of desert: some
billowy tall grasses, a puff of sagebrush, and one perfect Joshua tree.
She declares this is as the heaven she wants for you: Pillowy and pure,
here's a wilderness meant to frighten no one—not even you, Yiayia.

***

The Augusts
We were, admittedly, waiting for you to die
and I am in a city nowhere
near you when I get the call.

Then, as if in a dream sequence
I am in a museum, stopped at a painting
called *Lily and the Sparrows*

with its strange ancient baby at the window
with perfect translucent hands curved
like quarter-moons as you'd curve

your hands under running water
moving them right and left, in and out, swiveling
from your waist like a round washing machine with arms:

another idiosyncrasy. I want to keep
them all, pressed in this poem
like the stuck-flutter of *petaloudis.*

How you loved salmon-pink roses, the tiny lavender
moths flitting on the front lawn of your home
on 13th South. The dot punctuating each wing.

The whisper-rain of your prayers
spoken into the kitchen wall. Your face
far-off looking maybe into this day

when your own death hovers and draws
its fast, feathery, figure-eights in the air.
Because somehow when I think of you,

I think of birds, birds in their tinyness,
birds in their sharp faces
and your son-in-law, a man so gentle

that birds flew to his hands and were fed.
I think of how you envied my mother,
her fortune of fate, how she had grown to love her man so

that his touch sent the sparrows of her bloodstream
to scatter off the perches of her bones.
How once and for always, I would love a man

whose face was a bit like yours—a diamond-faced boy
with an aqualinear, slightly off nose with eyes the color
of your eyes *lathoprasina*—a mossy amber of olive oil and warm.

There was, in the blocky mass of his solid form, a certain
smallness to his stubborn shrug which makes me think then
that we've loved deeply we always somehow love

and look for it in the labyrinthine walls of museums
the fierce and fearful gaze.
Forgive me, Yiayia, for living your every unlived day.

For all the love you couldn't have, I've held one
extravagant as a murder, heiress to that sadness
that leaves me so grateful to be

at such a loss   that still   every elegy turns
to a love poem.   (I'm saying he left me)   to love even   his allergy
to sunlight,   the sneeze up into the sky   like a tiny accusation.

***

Forget kidneys—I have loved in such a way as to be willing to give up
organs I only had one of. I wish you that suffering—not griefless-
ness but a grief so rich it nearly crushes you. The heaven we in-
vent for you adds to that cloud-formed paradise: a cactus made of
cloud with needles so soft they give at your touch.

***

In the dream, another bird, soft water balloon of a body, greasy-dark
plus something green (how I want you) still and yet breathing. I
stay with it, there, praying breath by breath it survives. I wake be-
fore it dies or recovers.

***

The Augusts
Time takes me by the hand and walks me through the gypsy-songs
meant for you, meant to signal a summer's beginning but it's near
the end now. Love perches strange with its whirling wings stilled for a
minute and a matchstick body that looks minute but also—a wonder.
***

These days I want to believe in torpor in the place of any death.
Want to believe that she could keep her quiet heroics up: the way
she delivered my mother in front of the kitchen stove, standing,

her water breaking, the pain, a squat—then a babygirl caught
just before she hit the dirty floor. I thought she could always hold off
the death she'd refused for years.

***

The heaven I'd invent for you would be train cars full of roses and
    summer gypsies encamped at the water's edge. You, a small girl
    again, a donkey's back and your mother's arms on each side, that
    "snowed-in feeling" of safe and home as you loped down a hillside
    before hopelessness.

***

Somewhere in 1915, Marina Tsvetayeva writes of Osip Mandlestam
            No one has looked at you departing
            More tenderly, more irrevocably . . .
            I send you a kiss across hundreds
            of separating years.
In Russia, that same year, Marina farewells Osip before she knows the
    possible ending of their story. In Itea, you are a child, and every-
    thing is still possible.

***

The Russian—the Cyrillic squared and familiar
as the Greek penned on the air mail envelopes
bleeding purple on the Bible-pages of letters

that my father helped you write to your mother. The Gideon Bible
in the nightstand of the Woods Motel with its John 3.16 written out
in three dozen languages offered my first look at Russian

as I wandered into the familiar contours of letters I'd always known,
tried to sound out a meaning, then seasick: had my first glimpse
of how you must see the world, at once obvious and incomprehensible.

How well you know from its lack how language,
a fluency saves us. A paragraph of birds
on a half-dozen electrical lines tell a story

that could disperse with one difference in the air.
Your story was tattooed on the sameness of sky
that hung outside your window like a body.

***

Inside there is a chaos of sound, a crowd
of hateful voices and never a moment of peace.
But in the heaven I'd invent for you there is silence.
The voices gone. Your terror smothered
by the mattressed wall between the living and dead.
I wish for you nothing more extraordinary than the smell
of warm when the radiator kicks on that first night in late
October and I'm heating water for tea and I remember
you've been gone nearly two months now.
I haven't seen the hummingbird in over a month. It outlasted you
but not by much. It has become your bird: frantic,
a race of the heart, tuned to a hope for something sweet.
For some flower plucked straight from your best dream.
Yiayia mou—I wish for a mild forever to follow every flowering.
  for Asemoula Skouras Pavlos, 1910–2005

{

hers is a face always rising from water

the surviving twin always looking back

scooped out and braced against a fissured white sky

an earthworm drying after rain

a cartoon profile in a curtained window

the mosquito sting of her contour

a line drawing of regret by a lesser Picasso

her words are afterthoughts

a broken spine silhouette

her life held a breath

a secret in the spooned cave of the mouth

waiting to be filled in

she meant to be lightning

II

I measure every grief I meet.
EMILY DICKINSON

Baby, I suffer various degrees of wistfulness.
TERRANCE HAYES

LATHE

We were festooned with smoke and fire, with electrical storms.
Afterglow and math, death
in a ruby red bombshell wiggle dress.
We were divine interventions and leaking balloons.
We suffered from air loss and cabin pressure.
We suffered fevers of unknown origins.
We suffered farewells, divinities
sugary and ethereal. We suffered
    the disillusion of afternoon turned
like buttermilk to a dusk
rich as hand cream,
    the lotioned light
turned to lather
    and we washed away.
The gutters received us like messiahs
    then sent us on our way.

A chalk drawing of dissolution,
a cake of soap diminishing,
a cough drop in the rain.
We were breaking down like an old horse or a stain.

Recalling your skin of hard candy coffee-flavored.
Recalling your hands like pulled bulbs and the tension of roots.
Recalling those years like a faulty auto part or a hazard.

Turn this curve
    the mothwing cul-de-sac
    with intention
and some follow through. Or turn away.
    We're turning like sonnets
or inebriated dancers, we're turning
like milk and seasons
    sour.
    Directions to Aftermath Avenue:

Turn to the little yellow house
    where we lived a half-dozen winters ago
The Centipede Café we called it,
    for the false eyelash insects
    that skittered on floorboards.

Turn in the driveway, to where the road circles back.
The maple key in your palm that won't turn the lock,
turn a day or a leaf
    or a thing
turn back.

WHEN PLAYING BY THE BLUES

Light up. Your house or your life,
your photographs, no matter. Teach your baby
to wave goodbye. In the absence of your own
teach someone else's baby a cheap farewell
with one sweep nearly like erasing a board.
Now you can start. Write I am nothing
if not melancholy one hundred times
in cursive. From that imbroglio of text
weave something: hanging rope or safety net.
A walk-down, a levy up, a glissando
or a hopscotch all diagonal, until you see
in your melancholy, Baby, how funny
you are, all squinched up and sorrowful;
until you see *that's you* there sniffing the new blue roses
genetically engineered to smell like sky and grief
and August rivering into a fall
feeling too broken to play. Nevermind,
nevermind—the blues are meant for the broken.

BLUES TURNED TO BRUISE

Because color is not about what is, but what is desired.
PHIL PATTON, *ESQUIRE*, JULY 1995

These days you're the rage,
grape lollipop cars, aubergine bicycles,
eggplant taxicabs: *the new passion for purple.*

But it's not new to me. I knew you when
you were orphan hue, too whimsical for cars,
too fanciful for waiting rooms, too rich
for this, too flowery for that.

In an era overwhelmed with novelty
purple stands for persistence.

So that's how they're telling it now.
I knew you before yesterday's news
announced: *Man arrested for smuggling
rare eighteenth-century violins,*
and I was reminded of the woman
across the hall stalked by a violin
maker who whispers
into the receiver: *I'll carve you,
make you sing in keys
without names.*

She wasn't afraid,
didn't hear the way violins ring violence.
She heard only supple curves, richest wood
bending to his touch like leather,
stroked with a horsehair bow.
They say it's closest in sound
to the human voice.

The screaming strings,
high-pitched stirrings
we can't help ourselves.

Purple, yours is a complicated song
and I hear through your lavenders
and lilacs, *violet to violate,*
the way certain European men smoke
lips curled, a near disdain, cigarette flicked
in a motion swift and disregarding,
a little mean, lovely.
By all means, help yourself
when they ask for a light
and it's Friday afternoon
and your blood smells night
around the corner.

By all means,
I heard you then, percussive,
driving in the dark red mouths
of bruises humming the plum
gravel of the blues, the blue-red
neon hitting off, on, off
his mapped chest.

Help yourself,
your later voice, soothing
as I stared deep into the amethyst
ring I keep for a dose of you.

You are rooms full of blossom,
petals crushed into flesh: iris, amaryllis,
amaranth: the fuchsia flower,
which in legend never fades,
a lover's bloom.

I prefer roses—honest die-ers
the dusty lavonda,
tissue mauve so frail
even a touch undoes them.

MAKING RED

Meaning murderous

in a town so south
hot light steals the red
from azaleas & lipstick Corvettes.

Stop signs fade to an infected pink.

Salmon   Coral   Inflammation

We were caught red-handed
trying to take color back from the sun.

Vermilion   Red Ochre   Realgar

Our town was trying to ghost write itself
on every car that flashed through it.

Madder lake   Alizarin   Cinnabar

A sealing wax of scarlet lips
tongues the place where ache lives.
Your mechanical valentine
slips the tongue
         a paper cut/doll
                        wears a heart that moves
         this way
                        and that
with the slightest stroke   of your fingertip.

CADDIS FLIES IN TWO LESSONS

A complaint against being left behind while someone flits through Spain

1. Most caddis larvae surround themselves with a protective case made from various materials from their surroundings, fastened together with a sticky silk-like secretion produced from a gland near the mouth. Each species uses its own particular materials—grains of sand, plant fragments and even empty snail shells—and builds its case to a specific design. It is often possible to identify a species simply from its case. The sand grains or other materials are frequently cemented together very neatly to form a mosaic.

Postcard from Barcelona: *A weather report: The rain in Spain falls mainly on the plains.*

Reply from Alabama: *Here plain girls in print dresses drink rain from an unspained distillery.*

2. Moth-like insects with two pairs of membranous wings densely covered with tiny hairs and held roof-wise over the body at rest. All are fairly weak flyers and the females of a few species are wingless. Most are dull brownish or greyish insects, flying at dusk.

Postcards land in the mailbox I painted cool mint green:
The color of your favorite ice cream
(the color of your heart it seems).
They say *Lovely here, but missing you.*
They say *Every bright broken thing resounds with you.*
Or maybe simply *Wish I'd invited you.*
A drop of honey to each corner then I press
each postcard to my flesh until I am a Spanish panorama,
a caddis fly of fifty-cent sentiment.

Barcelona postcard: *If ever a city was your city . . . color upon color.*
A whether report: *Flightless girls find ways to flee.*
Spanish fly: *See anti-aphrodisiac. See Senorita Abandoned.*

Where you are the fountains spurt a collage of gaudy puzzles.
(Diviner, you helped me see pain in that country's name.)

Here I am a birdbath of spite.
A decoupage of longing.
A nude puzzle mostly undone.

If I could, I'd ask a passing caddis fly
if those gorgeous shards ever cut
the bodies they're meant to armor.

1. A Seeing Eye dog.
2. The better part of a decade.
3. A voluntary amnesia.
4. The better part of a heart.
5. The sky's cheap circus of sun up, sun down.
6. A stone fissured like an asterisk.
7. A blindfold made of cast iron.
8. What I could forgive.
9. Penny candy, old movies, a hundred dresses
     ten of them crinoline
                    thirty of them red.
10. Whatever I might've loved instead.

RECONSTRUCTING A BIRD

1.
If I drew your soul now
it would bring to mind Picasso's *Sigh*
an inked-in man, a wash of pale blue
near his abdomen, another near his mouth.

2.
In this one, she's walking after rain.
He's haunting an empty warehouse,
an abandoned home.
The sky is being refurbished
a scarf of cloud here
a peach full moon there
autumn dovetailing dusk.

3.
It's nearer thick blue, blurred-edge blue
lots of unforeseen in-between.
A glass elevator, a boy, a girl,
a seventy-three-story kiss.

4.
They've just stepped out of the club, steeped
in smoke, it's two A.M.
They're dressed-up: brocade jacket,
vintage necktie. Her mother's engagement
scarf circles her throat.
The jazz trio's a jukebox, request anything, it's yours,
says the cocktail waitress.
'Round Midnight murmurs
from the closed door.
He hums *I Mean You*
into her ear; it's late summer
they must be newly in love
and everything is in present tense.

5.
You again, taken from a second-story window
hands full of presents: a silver pencil, a thousand found pennies,
a handful of feathers, a cold cup of coffee.
With every bluejay feather he'll say:
Soon we'll reconstruct a whole bird
and I see it, bedraggled yet soaring
in a hush of glass-bottle blue.

THE DEAD MAGICIAN'S THINGS

For Nicholas, 1982–2001

I. They disappear on you anyway.
Warm weather comes and whisks them to beaches or summer jobs
and because you're young at this, you still caution
them at spring break to be careful with their bodies
on the road, in the water, on a binge.

The doomsayer said his name *Nicholas*
and his face rose from memory like a body
from a leaf-stained lake, from a flooded quarry
and the sharp features cut, and me just moments away
from teaching others and him, two years and nearly
two hundred students ago and later, some other boy not dissimilar
with that cutting, with eyes like wet stones and warmer.

Memorable—his mother asked what I might recall
if I had any old papers of his and I could only retrieve
a roll sheet with his signature, something
magical to it now. Any ink in his living hand
        a magic marker.
But there were others: I had nothing to give her
but these things belonged to him: the sunslant
at the window off his right shoulder, the radius of
a girl's perfume, the way the spider lily right
about now explodes into something part desperate hand,
part firework, the band of light
pooled on his lashes, the soda sizzle in his mouth,
the moth kiss of light snow, the world the world the world
and what it knew and would not know of him.

II. The dead magician's donated belongings.
    The cage of metal canisters nested,
ornamented with cheap bright pagodas
and men in funny hats, the seashell meant

to be hidden beneath one can then: sleight-of-hand trick
to make it so where things were once
they are no more, as with that dear vanished
boy, who I knew only slightly before the bitter
abracadabra of it all.

    I with no rights in this matter either.
Where was I?—teacher of nothing
he could use now—when he stepped off
this pulsating planet and away from the words
which I joked were almost always about dying
or love or loving the world and dying anyhow
and how that sucked—no more eloquence can reach
what I meant, or match her son, the mother who must now
feel like the magician's assistant, sawed-in-half, then revealed,
forced to amble across the stage: her life, as if whole again:
mother-of-Nicholas-for-always stuck there with a name
full of cuts and strikings shimmering the air
like a synesthetic moon left clanging
from the gong strike which was also my student
as he pierced that winter sky. That sky wearing all its heaven-ness,
a suit made large and of a synthetic fiber. But how it shone.

As did he—through so much confusion, the blur of students
so many of them but I recalled him—yes
just as he left—instantly.
And leaves me here, with words that can't retract
the awful truth of such a day
full of gravity's bright loss and so empty.
Which is this elegy, Nick,
and taking roll and toll all at once, your name written in
your now-miraculous hand to say
one day in cruel April you were *here*.
Who could've guessed it would mean so much?

You were not Jane thrown
from a horse, but your death threw
me through a Monday and back out into all of this
too much to bear, too much to spell out
even with the used magic I found donated
at the Goodwill Thrift Store and which I purchased
because you just never know.

SIGH

The blue breath of winter. The lake's promise
broken by a scribble of lightning.
The sundry all caves in, falls from grace,
the unglued tiles of heaven's mosaic rain
down bright glass darts on the fleshy city.
One grieving season hangs from a locket
off your neck, resting heavy at the throat.
The heart wants what it wants. So we say.
A still-life silhouette waves from the terrace.
A cough steps out on a frigid sidewalk,
city bus rolls past with an OFF-DUTY marquee;
Joy, the last soul on board, misses her stop.
The past hunkers down for a smoke.
Each breath bluer than the last.

CONTRE-COEUR

Let Nothing be that
which bitch-slaps the heart,
for the heart, like a hospital,
is a many-winged thing,

unlike Hope of the third floor,
the aging chanteuse with nodules on her vocal chords
which is to say, on the inside of her throat
(on the outside hangs a bedraggled feather boa).
In a few months, Hope will give up
singing, join a belly dancing troupe,
call herself Cymbrellina, wear chartreuse harem pants,
tops with a window for her tummy
to peer out at all the gardens of the city park,
where on a Sunday afternoon, the oaks, the swingset,
the children sway in time. Across the park

the tulips are playing country music,
some twang, a long drawl trailing like smoke
from each of their open gaudy mouths.
Under every tree a festival.

Somewhere in a diner
the old Hope makes circles
with the bottom of a water glass
until haloes chainlink the tabletop.
Shame on Hope, on sad, on every abstraction
that defies the belly dancers, their shimmies.

Let Nothing be that which smacks the heart—
that dumb fuck—around.
That bloody Morse code prattling all day long
but mutely so it can't be heard.
A lip-reader in the east wing knows the truth

about your lover's lover once-removed.
Whisper-slosh all you want, sly nightingale,
the heart's a bruiser in biker boots
with zero sense of humor, we're banding
together, we're on to you now.

ROMANCE IN CELADON

Verde que te quiero verde.
FEDERICO GARCÍA LORCA

How I want you, Green,
in the misty silver
of an olive grove.

Not emerald or peridot,
but chartreuse reverberation.
Not Day-Glo, but pure
    after-rain-in-a-wooded-place you.

They say you're a jealous one
    No other hue before me.
Purple has my heart, so you whisper through
tornado-whipped nights
when the sky wears you
darkwater and eerie
like a malignant olive frock.

Oh, what you do to eyes
bottleglass to juniper.
To wear you fatigued
in camouflage, an army's rage, or nostalgic
in a vintage smoking jacket, malachite,
a romaine scarf, an aged bruise—you're everywhere
a lush one. Any green light in a storm will do.

A woman tears through the jade jungle of you,
rests in your weedy garden, licks at your lime-flavored shade,
tastes your cool mint riverstones, tests the crabapple skin,
just to hear your feather fern tongue flirt with the wind,
your velvet mouth, your verdant voice:
Hang with me in a dangerous sky

weave through trellis with me.
Let us tangle under a tropical, mean-hearted
seawater awning.

Just say you love me best.

Say it, and she'd try, wistfully thinking: violet, heliotrope, lavender.
Say you love me best.
Old wounds, lost limbs, lichen, moss agate, ivy-eyed felines,
parakeet plumage, pines, everything pines.
    You could be the one she learns to love best.
Forest in his father's old suit. Sage in a leaf-thin dress.

ANY OLD MIRACLE

We met on the street that last time holding
cups of tepid coffee.
You were wearing dove
    grey. We turned the corner
and a fortuneteller called out: *You there,   listen.*
I knew someone once, a young woman like you. Listen,
her palm held a thousand secrets, a hundred deaths,
a million hearts or more. I read the story of time between
her wrist and the bone of her thumb. I saw all there was to see
about light in the slim lines braceleting her hand, the beginning
of the world in the wrinkles of her little finger.
    And love? I told her everything about love that day
we kept walking until her voice thinned
to the end of the block,
then slipped down the stairs
    behind the clouds
into the cracks   of our crumbling   sidewalk
and you laughed   a bright laugh
full of tangerines   glitter   rain.

HOT LUNCH POEM

Dear little Roman god of skewed seeing,
Check the eye chart and get back with me
                    URZ1
                 OUOY

Dear Willing Misbeliever, the only hotel
key to our story's in Romania.
You've grabbed the wrong clues
and the wrong crimes
and run past the jury with them.

I would have chased you down (forgive me?)
but I was busy
hanging from
the gallows
in the town
square
of your used-
to-be heart.

Drop that key like a gun
into the nearest mailbox
where it can unlock
something tangible.

Whoever puts a hand
on you now should do
so as if you're
a stealable good
in an Arab market.

You are a stealable good,
aren't you, Moonpie?

My anti-theft devise is a machete.
Your anti-theft devise is a machete.
The clock hands are twin machetes.

Dear Victim of Every Single Thing,
Dear Lunch of My Life, let bygones be begonias
growing from the tip of each finger.

I'm so cross with you,
I'd like to smash your glasses.

My front door bears a ring of dead flowers
as a porthole frame for your nowhere little face.
My wind chimes cry out in your honor.
My forearm remembers the exact heft and heat
of your abdomen against it.

The man who asks for spare
change told me
I was the saddest
girl in the gaslight district,
and Dearest Tongue Depressor,
without running a single census
you can bet that it's true.

The world is too much without
us and tables run like trains
in the all-you-can-eat buffets
that once made you cry.
We're the tables laden
with our every misplaced hunger.
The sun has shed at least one skin
since the last time you touched me,
wars started, babies were born to be given
the names of dead Russian poets

and there's a new strain
of flu this year—more sickening than ever.
Whole gardens of stars will die between us.
A tree branch brushes up against a planet
and a sprinkle of coruscation makes
the road between us into a glitzy bridge.
Come here, Daffodil, there's too much
of everything, but nothing
in the way of love.

INTAGLIO

(a love song for the living dead)

My Sweet   engraveable You
depressed below the surface   smooth to the touch
        saddest at that
                            carving
craving elision
so that an impression
by design yields   a cameo afloat
            you are what you are not
an image in relief   composite of
loss
        re-leaf   what a good tree does
reel off   one good reason   one last fish
real if
        you're loved
            says the velveteen rabbit

real if
    you're ending
            your rending   a remnant collage

        I know a Paradise when I see one, because I've seen one.
        The trick is now to see another till I see One again.

the sunken treasure
                                    of a semiprecious life
        vitreous   excised from inside
which is to say brittleness + luster
                            I've entangled with the dying
                light
            think tango

the big dip
(One)   per lifetime
                              my drop-dead Lovely
           prized-consolation   kisses goodbye
the art or process of executing
                                        the art of losing
                                        just enough
printing (die-stamping & gravure)
done from   (done for)

the image sunk below
                        the surface
                  lowering the body
                                    (absentee voter)
formed from emptiness

Beauty has three possible endings and only one of them is bearable.

I mean   cut into
which is to say   taken from
cut it out
                        the five points of a body
                  star or human doll
cut from the flat felt of skyscapes
     by this I mean
those people-shaped places in midnight
                        traveling twice light's speed
     (half godspeed)

Captain Valentine will do everything possible to avoid turbulence.

a shoebox full of hope   & sweet minutiae
           tucked under one arm
kindly re-soul me   & please
           reupholster this fabric
everafter with

                    more minutes
less gauzy heaven-cloth
                        & some rich soil
a soft landing   an impression
from earth I would like
something of a garden   (she grew basil from seed for you)
        sole paradise   served whole
won't hold us   so hold On(e)

Been a long time crossing that bridge of sighs
been a long time crossing sings
a man like Byron, half in love with what may or may not
be the near-dead strolling from palace to prison and back,
but just a man on a covered bridge
being moved from here to there.

There
is no last sigh
if what you mean is intentional intake and relinquishing, a bridge
of sorts. There is another way the body sings
a swan song. A secret breath it holds back
until the soul's well on its way to the world, not

of this world, and not
really *there* if you mean there
in the way a river is there, or say, a way back.
The dead sigh is a function of air and slow collapse of lung.
    The sighs
we hear are from the survivors. The dead cease
to regret. (Or so we pray). The bridge

as Byron pointed out is an enclosed bridge
between palace and prison, but it is not
a bridge between life and the moments we seize
for a lyrical ending. Still I'd like to imagine us there,
holding hands with the doomed, walking through beauty so
    sharp it sighs
—and we sigh back.

The view isn't really the last thing they look back
for or from. Because the bridge
was built *after* the executions ended. That's the size
of it. But I prefer Byron's telling, before I knew that it was not
a last glance to the water, the city, the air
so bright-burning beautiful it must singe

the eye and the heart about to sing and then un-sing
everything it ever loved and lost. Back
to a place before there
was a man crying. *Been a long time crossing this bridge*
of sighs. Before there was even a body (and not
a bridge) built of sighs

or stone. It's this mundane. The dead sighs leave the body like birds
   bored with the place they chose to light.
There, I like to imagine just the sighs whisper-soft-shoeing, as sighs
   must brush against a stone bridge with steps so light, they leave no
   echo, not one last breath to sing back
   the tale of us and just how it goes.

BLACK POWDER

picked up at the train station
by the son of a plantation owner
waist-high in the Black Belt

Hundreds of night-filled sacks arrived
Bags of darkness enough to blow
a whole mossy crow-swarmed
ravine into nightfall

Those boys struck the matches
lit the trail at dusk

The horizon shook
ink trees scratched at the sky for a way out
and then scribbled themselves into oblivious designs

A thousand crows rose
in smoke gales
then downed themselves
swift like shots of sloe gin

the arcs of them bad boomerangs
eyebrows raised in a thousand gestures
of bewilderment then dropped

for days ashes hung like Spanish moss

III

What wouldn't we have given for a life of ordinary heartbreak?
NADEZDHA MANDELSTAM

Marina we were late. Marina we were early. I love you.
KENNETH KOCH

MARINA TSVETAYEVA RESPONDS TO A PRESENT-DAY PARAMOUR WRITING FROM THE FRENCH QUARTER

Listen now, mundane as they may be, I am formed by love and loss whatever better place to dwell on or in, I could never make home there. But I could never make home anywhere. I was a vagabond to this planet at best. You said the same thing, didn't you, about the past and memory's long shadow that casts nowhere long enough to cool a single burning day.

I knew a picture hanger like you, once. He only believed in a world under glass. What he loved he framed, what he framed he hung up across the room from his favorite chair. His was an orderly, well-designed life. When you say I rhapsodize, I believe, Sir, you are accurate.

I think I should like to spend a lifetime rhapsodizing—even lost love, even nature—especially the human variety. Where I live is not where I live, if that address is planet Earth. You're right to say mine is a heart-driven landscape, but something must drive any spirit and I was here once, and I was burning. I was force then and fire. How many can say the same?

I have received the dozen broken glass flowers. As for the absinthe, set up the sugarcube and the slotted spoon. I only trust that which breaks down just to take you away with it.

Tartly,

Marina T.

FOUND POEM, LOST GIRL, 1918
Ariadna Efron, Age 6, Writes of Her Mother, Marina Tsveteyeva

My mother is very strange. My mother is not at all
like a mother. Mothers always admire their child
and children generally, but Marina does not like little children.

She has light brown hair; it curls up at the sides.
She has green eyes, a hooked nose, and pink lips.
She has a slender build and arms which I like.
Her favorite day is Annunciation Day.
She is sad, quick, and loves
Poems and Music.
She writes Poems.

She is patient and tolerant
to the extreme. Even though she gets angry
she is loving. She is always hurrying somewhere.
She has a big heart. A gentle voice. A fast walk.
Marina's hands are full of rings.

Marina reads at night. Her eyes are nearly always full
of fun. She does not like being pestered with silly questions,
then she gets very angry.

Sometimes she walks about like someone lost,
but then she suddenly seems to wake up,
starts to talk, and again seems to go
off somewhere.

ORDINARY HEARTBREAK

*Ariadna Efron to Anna Akhmatova upon the occasion
of her mother, Marina Tsvetayeva's, death*

Poetess. I think you are right to despise the word.
It sits too high in the trees and what comfort
is it to widows and orphans?

Six days before my thirtieth birthday
my mother's shoes hung three feet from the ground,
around her neck, a ring of darkest blue.

By now you've heard, Anna.
I'm the daughter of a late storm-spooked mare
with beautiful hair and viscous eyes
thick green as virgin olive oil
sad, deep-set, heavy-lidded as yours.

I'm foreign to my name, *Ariadna,*
translated in her voice as *Alya.*
Hers is the name I always hear in script: *Marina.*

Without her the days clash with everything.
I confuse things—your words, my mother's voice.
I dream her meeting my father in a grove
and telling him to wait, telling him:
    You will leave anyway, so why not now?
    The bad fruit falls; I have put out a lantern
    and washed the windows because you glimmer
    in the light like a rare fish,
    because you are ghostly and unresolved.
They say she died with a tiny blank notebook
sewn into her dress, a pencil, sharp, frail as birdbone,
tied on a loop through the hinges.
I want to believe she's on her way,

on a late train, reading in the night,
her hands covered in rings, silver bracelets,
strands of Bohemian glass
around her neck.

And for you, Anna, a letter.
    A fresh, dark elderberry branch in the mail.

Or a torn, dirty postcard in her hand:
    Listen, Anna, who cares
that the miraculous comes just so close then turns
a corner, finds a place to disappear?
Who cares about the ruined city, poems about air
and heroes, the lilac mists of empty gardens?
Who cares whether we wrote it down
or knew those dark ashes by heart?
Someone should.

DEAR RAINER MARIA RILKE,

My mother swallows fire for a living. Each angel burns to know as much as you knew of death long before you found your way there. Which is why I write you now, seven hours after they've cut my mother's body down from the rope that leads to where you are, dead as anything, excepting of course those angels—ashes they must be or so hot to the touch that no one gets near them and they stay shiny as the day they were made. No one fingerprints them. Nothing leaves proof on their bodies of any contact. Bruiseless, surely they mourn.

My mother swallows fire for a living or she writes poems, we're always confusing the two.

My mother walked into every room open as any waterfall. From her letters you know that just as you know my name—the daughter from the poem. The last, living, left-behind one. Tell her, won't you, Rainer, I might've liked to love her as you have—from a distance. Her letters coming to you like death in waves. I'm asking you to meet her. Remind her: every angel burns. Tell her I'll look for her whenever I smell flesh on fire or drag my fingers across the kind of skin that feels thick like gardenia petals. I'll look for her in women shaped like scorched angels or angels shaped like girls and I'll taste their mouths to see if what lingers there is smoke or vinegar and by that I'll know her.

Tell her I know why. Use your words, Rainer, that to stay is to be nowhere and thirsty walking on the outskirts of the villages of ourselves where even further out we see a pond set just exactly one step too far for a drink. To stay is to be nowhere and numb where a tree might grow on us for all we'd notice and there—a chandelier of white tears flower off our left shoulders.

Every angel burns—sunscreen and wing. My mother's on her way. Arm her if you're willing. Dodge her if you must. Give her bouquets of elegies. Remind her that she died in gravity's hold and that I'm here still, held by that same pin.

Ariadna Efron

From an obituary translated online from Russian.

Ariadna Sergueevna Efron
(1912–1975), the girl of Marina
Tsvetayeva, was born in
Moscow. In 1922, she
accompanied her mother in
emigration. She made
secondary studies with the
Russian college in
Czechoslovakia, and her
studies higher than Paris, the
School of the Louvre and the
School of the Applied Arts. She
collaborated in newspapers
published by the Soviet
embassy and France-USSR
association. In 1937, she
returned to Moscow and
worked there as journalist and
illustrator with the Union of the
newspapers and reviews. In
1939, she was stopped and
condemned to eight years of
camp. Having purged her
sorrow, she settled in 1947 in
Riazan, and taught in a school
of art. In 1949, she again was
stopped and condemned to the
exile in the area of
Krasnoïarsk. She was
rehabilitated in 1955. She
devoted the twenty last years of
her life to the literature.

NEARER VENUS
Letter from the Other Side of the Sky

Ten Years after Her Own Death, the Late Ariadna "Alya" Efron Receives Word That Astronomers Are Naming a Crater on Venus after Her Mother, Marina Tsvetayeva

Oh Marina,

   If it's true—as you've said—that the dead are faithful—how will that faith look on you? Like a dress being worn for the first time? Faithlessness being the greater part of Marina, that and your sterling trinkets, and your weathery wheat-colored hair that reeked of wanderlust.

It comes as no surprise that they're naming a crater on Venus after you. A hole on the planet of love and beauty. A planet with a hole in its heart. Your own heart a mesh of lacunae, pitted affection. The planet without satellites. You, too, a planet that could carry no moons.

Loving you was loving that which ached to hold: Broken glass in the pocket. Broken glass in the mouth.

Your friends described you as a mist-wreathed nun, a single naked soul with salty peasant eyes. Grey eyes—the color of ambivalence. A favorite of the faithless. Isn't it? Even I told the biographers when they asked that you were able to subordinate any concerns to those of your work—I insisted *any*—I meant it then as I do now.

Even as child I understood that attachments were too much for you to carry or carry for long. *It was I who once shattered my every happy love*—your words again.

I write to say I *almost* understand: You were down to one loaf of bread, down one daughter, one husband, countless lovers.

Oh Mother of an unrhymed universe, I'm glad a bit of sky bears your name. There are no small craters there, but it is the brightest planet. I wish I'd seen it just once from Earth. From such a beautiful distance it might make sense of everything—might make a lit mobile, bright wind chimes of all those disuniting years I carried long after you floated from the rafters of memory.

MARINA RESPONDS TO HER ELDEST DAUGHTER

Ariadna, you are memory's child
more than my own. Misremembered
you'll find me where the Russian sky
is stitched to the revolutionary earth.

We were all walking wounded then.
Always wintering, always cold-
blooded as we had to be.

Engraved as you are with my absence,
my name, my ways,
a woman's body holds sway
over you. Recall me
to the measured world as writer first,
woman second,
a mother somewhere
down the line.

But I *loved* you, my oldest, my left-behind
lantern girl burning in her paper walls.

Thirty pieces of silver mark betrayal everywhere
so everyone spoke of your starved sister,
the brutal winters, and my hands covered
in coldest sterling bands.

To that, how can I say anything
mother-spoken and generous?

I tried to leave you the way
dew leaves the olive leaves
slowly and under a great spell of sun.

Think of me as half there, not gone, a raped star,
deadly and bright burning to my death.
Think of me as a stunned-planet. Unsunned.

I ABSOLVE YOU, MARINA TSVETAYEVA

Remember, Marina, you were just a girl who vowed
to take any beam of light she saw
and trapeze out
before darkness swung back.

A world away from you and that heartless climate
    you called home,
one dreary season lit into the next
    and here we try to be content enough with fair weather,
a friend's wedding, or the fact that we're insured—so to speak.

Still there are skies we will never see again.
Certain comets will blaze on without us
and eclipses with their slow burlesque.
There are various ways of making
the moon and sun undress
    and they outlast us all.

The sky's magician pulls scarves of air
from sleeper's throats and the sky
stays hung with that pre-dawn gauziness.

So if the air we woke to each morning
weren't crowded with last night's last breaths
we might've turned from a flat-out miracle with ease.

Now we wait for the flowering of some fire
to burn a color we've only seen in dreams
like exploding candles—a geyser of wax
—that so-needed crayon rain
and what it stains or scalds matters barely.

Know the moon will not gutter in such a sky
but will burn and burn
off the toxic paint in the lobbies

of every dilapidated hotel in heaven
where, Marina, you wait in thinnest limbo.

And all that about tenderness and what to do about it.
The biographers said that when you said *eyelash*
you meant Mandelstam.
So they were everywhere like centipedes
    your lashes *your lashes* (damn them) *longer than anyone's.*
All that tenderness piling up in snowbanks.

Eyelashes encoding beloveds—all those ridiculous poems
collecting lashes like cosmic debris,
like cinders, like that;
    the lashes his, the heart yours,
that was said to be too large
or too small depending on the weather,
on how you washed it
    down. I understand. From here, where even
the trees are dropping limbs
on any willing surface and languishing,
I've a lashy boy of my own, and words by the kilo,
and they serve me like they served you,
with bent knees and filmy blades of resentment.
But I don't let up. Like trees
we'll lay it all down for the paper
or one hard storm or a good fringy set of eyes,
and there's no point in being sorry for that
here on this planet with the sky forgetting us
    even before we're gone.

So what if across town and alone
your husband's candle burned lower
and longer into the night,
afraid to lean into anything for fear
of burning everything down?

I mean, there are skies that will never see us again, Marina.
Unless they don X-ray glasses ordered from the back
of some comic book and peer hard at the ground
that holds us like a cough drop on its dry tongue.

Even that much isn't guaranteed.
You, Sister with a stone marking the patch of ground
    you *meant* to be sleeping in.
Instead they buried you elsewhere—more proof
that we should lie wherever we want while we can.

Once on a Friday on a garbled answering machine
wasn't it your voice I heard, Marina?
    A deep freeze and without food.
    My husband imprisoned, my starving children.
    Call it protective coloring, emotional camouflage.
    Call it survival because it was.

    In that frozen Russia, I was nothing less
    than an adaptive beast, sick with war and winter
    cold and able to slip
    into the state of being that would fill me.
    The men, the women nourished me.
    I mean, I'd fall in love. I saved myself
    as long as I did by staying so full I needn't eat,
    so feeling I couldn't even touch myself.

REASONS I GAVE FOR GIVING IT UP

Because I hung it in the window
and the sunlight robbed it of color
Because I left it under the care of an amnesiac
Because it did me
Because it did me in
Because it was not mine by law
Because I hung it in the window
and it robbed the sun of color
Because it regained memory and told everything
Because I filtered every loss through it
and it cast fanged shadows
Because it was unwieldy and wild to the bone
Because it recoiled from my touch
Because it rubbed against me
Because it outlasted the others by a longshot
Because it shattered underneath the bed
and imbedded itself in the soles of my feet
Because it cut me to the quick
Because it bled me
Because it asked nothing of me
Because I lived for it and asked too much
Because I left it for dead

And sorry I was though
I blew it out like a candle.
And sorry I was though
I whipped it like a meringue
and made a sweet pie of it.
And sorry I was though
I took it into my lungs
made a ring of smoke
and released it as a full white zero
into the July air.
And sorry I was though
the starry sky claimed it in a single inhalation
as if it had never been there.

CASTANET

Begin by dying.
Remove the velvetiest fruitflesh
from yesterday. Listen for ripeness.

Outside people plan parties,
weddings. They chisel ice.
They carve cakes. They throw flowers.
Their mouths move toward the motions of meaning.
The people say nothing
for a long time.
Then say even more.

Tune the spheresongs to the exact pitch
of musicbox nerve-endings where the room opens
its brace-tinselly mouth and you spill out   pulling yourself
from yourself   a magician's veil,
the throat of winter   a visible cough
scarfs the neck of the city,
a starlet gazes off a billboard
with candelline eyes. Aquarium hours and dim
thicknesses of light and air. All music muffled now.
The moon suggests no man, no rabbit
but a woman holding a fan
and turning away.

Cast a net for your own lost magic.
Spell yourself back in sign language
to the palm of your hand.
Drive to Demopolis or the town
where surely the biggest ball of yarn
waits ungodly and displayed
(more dumb matter). Jewelbox turtles
with their marcasite eyes blink a message so coded,
so crucial you close your eyes. Circle mouths
of fish call up to you. Someone has filled a cast-metal-supermarket

gumball-machine with fish food, and now it winks
a bright lever at you and you what *can* you do?
Drop a wafer coin into the slot, turn the steel crank, and feed
them until the day burns itself away.
Like kites on a string, a chain of fish swim by,
pendants on a borrowed wrist of sky.
Make use of these spells: maracas rattle through dried leaves
down evening avenues you've never known.
Some hours are an Easter basket.
The sky is a charm bracelet.

DAMASKED

Meet my old mistress

meet my new mistress,   just the same
meet my love   for my new mistress flashier

meet my new life
continually revised

an unmended fence
the gaps

the thing is

la bella luna

but what suffers

mistresses to harem

aren't her eyes exactly
like the sun
but brighter?
or duller depending
on what she wears

oddly unrevised or
infinitely broken

with strays flying in through

you can tell two stories

la luna bella

what falls out that can't be
regathered

flower to bouquet

A sum of their parts

arrange us like flowers

even Mary the contrary one

any rung to hold her

each mistress calls out

aches for a ladder

she's ready to climb

EULOGY FOR A MOURNING CLOAK BUTTERFLY

Dearly Beloved
we are scattered here
like anywhere
raging against
the radiator
whose cry
kept us awake
night after night after
our wings
brittled our hearts
folded into news
paper ship hats
delivered as a cape
of great sorrow
no matter the address
attended every trumpet
flower loved to flitter
remember thusly best to wear
one thing well
in lieu of flowers   flowers

GLEAN

You maybe haven't seen it in my eyes,
that's all right by the wren's cry, all right by me.

There is this heron in a hush of lift
and my eyes are filled with it

plus the plumage of a thousand waterbirds
add the damage of the cat's teeth as they mouth words

to birdflesh, as they speak afterglow and loom
and journey out and arc away as to go luminous

in your going as to go out to where the us
trees don't grow, out to the bus stop

carved in stone where a mineral mother
clutches a rock baby until her arms crumble.

She maybe hasn't seen the marquis pupil
of the sorry catseye, the long gleam, the star's key

that unlocks the nightsky, lets out a ream of morning
paper, the light off the sun. A scream forming

at the back of dawn's throat ripples out
a stone's throw from the stone woman, the infant

clutched in a blanket carved from rock, each fold
holds a river of history cemented and old, colder

than the bird's rush over silver water,
the granite woman, her petrified daughter.

You see I meant to mention the loon
mournful and mooning, a sound still burning

from the empyrean room, an altitude beyond us.
The loon bids goodbye with every note sung.

NOTES

PART I: The epigraph is used in Anne Sexton's poem "Suicide Note." It appears to have been a quotation from an anonymous late-nineteenth- or early-twentieth-century will.

FERNANDO PESSOA, I SALUTE YOU ALL: The epigraph is from Edwin Honig's translation of the poem, "Maritime Ode," written as Pessoa's heteronym, Alvaro Campos. "Here, there, everywhere you" is from Campos's poem "Tobacco Shop."

EPITHALAMIUM FIFTY-FIVE YEARS AFTER THE FACT OF YOUR SADDEST DAY: In Greek, *Yiayia* is "grandmother."

A HUMMINGBIRD FEEDER SHAPED LIKE A STRAWBERRY: In Greek, *petaloudis* is "butterflies" and *mou* is "my."

INTAGLIO: The "Paradise" quotation is by Donald Revell. The "Beauty" quotation is by Larry Levis. "Captain Valentine" refers to an anonymous flight attendant on flight 1431 from Chicago, Illinois, to Salt Lake City, Utah.